YAS

21ST CENTURY DEBATES

RACISM

THE IMPACT ON OUR LIVES

CATH SENKER

Raintree

Chicago, Illinois

21st Century Debates Series

Genetics • Surveillance • The Internet • The Media • Artificial Intelligence • Climate Change • Energy • Rain Forests • Waste, Recycling and Reuse • Endangered Species • Air Pollution • An Overcrowded World? • Food Supply • Water Supply • World Health • Global Debt • Terrorism • The Drug Trade • New Religious Movements • Violence in Society • Tourism • Transportation and the Environment

© 2003 Raintree

Published by Raintree, a division of Reed Elsevier Inc., Chicago, Illinois

For information, address the publisher:
Raintree, 100 N. LaSalle, Suite 1200, Chicago, IL 60602

Library of Congress Cataloging-in-Publication Data:
Senker, Cath.
  Racism / Cath Senker.
    p. cm. -- (21st century debates)
Summary: An exploration of the history and contemporary issues of racism with a focus on finding methods to solve the problem.
Includes bibliographical references and index.
  ISBN 0-7398-6467-X (Library Binding-hardcover)
  1. Racism--Juvenile literature. [1. Racism.] I. Title. II. Series.
  HT1521.S38 2004
  305.8--dc21

                        2003002172

Printed in Hong Kong.

Picture acknowledgements: Howard Davies/Exile Images 22, 28; Eye Ubiquitous 24 (David Cumming); Impact Photos cover, 9 and 17 (E. Andrews), 51; Mary Evans Picture Library 10; Popperfoto 4, 6, 8 (Ian Waldie), 14, 15, 16, 27 (Jerry Lampen), 36 (Will Burgess), 39 (Rula Halawani), 42 (Shannon Stapleton), 44 (Dimitar Dilkoff), 45 (Enny Nuraheni), 46 (Faith Saribas), 52 (Dwight Andrews); Rex Features/Sipa Press 48 (Ilyas J. Dean), 50, 37 (Benoit Schaeffer); Topham 5, 13, 18 (Press Association), 20 (Jeff Greenberg), 21 (Bob Daemmrich), 31, 32, 33, 35, 38, 41 (David Wells), 54, 55, 58, 59.

Cover: foreground picture shows a 1988 demonstration in France by the far right; background picture shows a march against the apartheid government in Durban, South Africa.

Acknowledgements:
The author would like to acknowledge www.tolerance.org for information on the right wing in the United States, and the Australian Human Rights and Equal Opportunity Commission for information on racism and human rights in Australia.

CONTENTS

WHAT IS RACISM?

FACT

In 1914 the British Empire had a population of 431 million people, of whom 60 million were white people governing themselves, including Great Britain itself. This meant that Britain ruled over 370 million nonwhite people.

What is "race" anyway?

Throughout modern history, there have always been people who have said that human beings can be divided into different races. Some have claimed that having a black or a white skin can make a difference in a person's intelligence and abilities. For example, a Swedish botanist in the 1700s, Carolus Linnaeus, divided human beings into six "races." The 18th-century British philosopher David Hume wrote that black people were naturally inferior to white people.

Misguided anthropologists in the 1800s measured skulls to classify people by race. They claimed that black people were the closest to our ape ancestors and white people the most advanced. These studies were used to justify colonial rule by white people over black and Asian people. Several Victorian writers, including historian Thomas Carlyle and English novelist Anthony Trollope, also expressed the view that colonialism was in accordance with the "natural order."

An 1888 portrait of British philosopher Herbert Spencer

No basis in science

In the mid-1860s, a scientist named Herbert Spencer came up with the phrase "survival of the fittest" to describe how animals compete with each other to survive in the natural world. Some scientists tried to relate this idea to human society. They argued that those who did well in the world were stronger specimens of the human race. Since white people controlled vast sections of the globe, this supposedly indicated that they were stronger and smarter than those they ruled over.

It has now been proven that the concept of race has no basis in science. Within human beings there are huge variations in physical appearance. For example, only 6 out of a total of 30,000 genes in the human body account for all the differences in skin color in Europe and Africa. This means that so-called "racial" differences are literally skin deep. It has also been proven that there is no link whatsoever between so-called "racial" variations and intelligence.

This group of students at the State University of New York may have different skin colors, but their color tells us nothing about their intelligence, interests, habits, or customs.

VIEWPOINTS

"The negroes are made on purpose to serve the whites, just as the black ants are made on purpose to serve the red."
View held by Thomas Carlyle and Anthony Trollope, summed up in The Spectator *magazine, Britain, 1865*

"When gene geography [looking at the genes of people in different places] is used to look at overall patterns of variation, it seems that people from different parts of the world do not differ much on average. Color does not say much about what lies under the skin."
Steven Jones, The Language of Genes, *1993*

Today, sociologists talk about ethnicity rather than race. They consider that groups of people have different cultures, languages, customs, and ways of life that make them part of a particular ethnic group. Yet race still does have a meaning today, because society gives it a meaning. When certain groups are valued less than others and are treated badly, then race becomes a real issue.

Prejudice

A black woman in New York City calls the police because her front door is being kicked in by racists. Members of her family are beaten up. The police don't turn up for three days. In the streets of Dublin, an Irish man yells at a Kosovan asylum seeker. He tells him to go home and stop taking Irish people's jobs. A Maya woman in Guatemala has waited for hours at the hospital with her sick baby, but all the nurses seem to be ignoring her.

In 1999 thousands of Maya held a peaceful demonstration in Guatemala, demanding land and better living conditions.

In all these examples, racism is at work. Racism starts with prejudice. People who are prejudiced decide what they think about someone based on what group that person comes from. People can be prejudiced against all kinds of groups. For instance, older people might be prejudiced against young people with piercings and dyed hair, thinking they are all troublemakers.

Some people are prejudiced against a group of people because of their skin color, ethnic group, religion, or culture. They have negative feelings that are not based on facts about that group. This is racism. For example, in Guatemala there is prejudice against the indigenous Maya people. Many Guatemalans think the Maya are stupid and primitive, because they follow a more traditional lifestyle.

Stereotypes and discrimination

If people think that something is true of a group of people in general, this is a stereotype. There are many kinds of stereotypes, usually negative and insulting. For instance, young people may think that all old people are traditional and boring. Some people are stereotyped because of their religion, skin color, or culture. In the United States, immigrants are often stereotyped as criminals who are cheating the welfare system to gain benefits.

When a particular group of people is treated worse than other groups because of their ethnicity, religion, or culture, this is discrimination. The police who didn't show up when the black woman called them discriminated against her family. They didn't take the complaint seriously, perhaps because they didn't believe the people under attack were important. If a white family had been attacked by a gang of black youths, might they have arrived on the scene sooner?

VIEWPOINT

"I am of East Timorese background. The police automatically think I am a drug dealer when they see me walking in the street. I am sick of being asked for ID [proof of identity]."
East Timorese man, Australia, 2001

DEBATE

Do people of similar backgrounds or cultures always get along better? Or is it true that "opposites attract"?

Types of racism

A variety of forms of racism exists in society. In school you might have heard students using racist nicknames or telling racist jokes. They might say that they are just joking and don't mean to hurt anyone. But it is no fun for the people being teased. It can encourage more racist remarks and make school a frightening place for them.

The Finsbury Park Synagogue in North London is seen through a broken window after it was vandalized in April 2002.

Groups of people may call others names because of a stereotyped view they have of them, such as the example of the Kosovan asylum seeker on page 6. This is called verbal abuse. Others may go further and attack the property of the group they hate. In March 2002 in Marseilles, France, a synagogue was burned to the ground, a horrific act that had not occurred since the Nazis were in power in the 1940s. A month later, anti-Semites attacked a synagogue in London, drawing a Nazi swastika and smearing excrement on the walls.

Some people may even attack another person purely because of their skin color, ethnic group, or religion. For example, in April 2000 Richard Scott Baumhammers killed three immigrants in Pittsburgh, Pa. Apparently he wanted to form a political party opposed to immigration.

Institutional racism

In Western countries, nonwhite people generally live in poorer housing and are paid lower wages than white people. This happens because of institutional racism. Even though racism is against the law, the way that society is organized means that certain minorities are treated unfairly. This unequal treatment means that it is hard for people from those minority groups to break out of poverty and thrive in the world. For instance, in the United States the level of unemployment for African Americans has been roughly twice that of white people since 1954. African-American women are also four times more likely than white women to die while giving birth.

Sometimes a country adopts racism as its official policy. In South Africa under the apartheid regime (from 1948 to the early 1990s) the law discriminated against nonwhite people. In cases like this, racism infects the whole of society.

FACT

Racism can be directed against white people as well as black people. For instance, in Europe there is discrimination against asylum seekers from the Balkans and eastern Europe, even though they are white.

DEBATE

If someone at school tells a racist joke, does that make the person a racist?

Segregation is shown on a sign on a beach in the Western Cape, South Africa, under the apartheid regime. Under apartheid, black people had to use separate, inferior facilities to those used by white people.

HISTORY OF RACISM

VIEWPOINT

"Historically, it is pretty well proved now that the ancient Greeks and Romans knew nothing about race. They had another standard—civilized and barbarian—and you could have a white skin and be a barbarian, and you could be black and civilized."

Historian C. L. R. James, 1973

Has racism always existed?

Throughout ancient and medieval history, there was prejudice against people who were seen as different. In the days when few people traveled, it was normal to distrust outsiders, even if they were from a different part of the same country. Dislike of foreigners was very common. This is called *xenophobia*, a Greek word meaning "fear of strangers."

Certain minority groups and people of different religions also suffered from prejudice. For instance, Jewish people were forced to flee from the ancient land of Palestine in the second century C.E. after they were crushed by their Roman rulers. They fled to North Africa and Turkey and later to western Europe. In medieval times they were expelled from those countries, too. Between 900 and 1100 C.E., tens of thousands of Christian soldiers joined the Crusades, crossing Europe on their way to conquer Jerusalem for the Christians. During their march, they murdered both Jews and Muslims.

This 19th-century Spanish print shows a crusader as a hero of the Christian Church, riding a white horse and wearing a halo. He is killing and trampling on Muslims in the name of his religion.

The nature of racism

Has racism always been the same or has it changed over time? There are different theories about this. One opinion is that racism has always existed in human society. Some people of color believe that the problem is white society and culture. There is something in white people's heads that means that they will always hate people of color. In the United States, Louis Farrakhan, leader of the Nation of Islam since 1978, has said that for this reason African Americans should live separately from white society, developing their own economy and resources.

Yet another view is that modern racism began when European traders started to exploit Africa, South America, and Asia for resources and slaves. It was developed to justify exploiting nonwhite people. From the 1700s onwards, as European countries took over foreign lands as colonies, modern racism became the justification for empire-builders to mistreat the people in their colonies. In recent times, it has developed into racism against immigrants.

A map shows colonial powers and the colonies they controlled in the late 1800s. Semicolonial states, such as Turkey, Iran, and China, were run by local rulers in alliance with a colonial power.

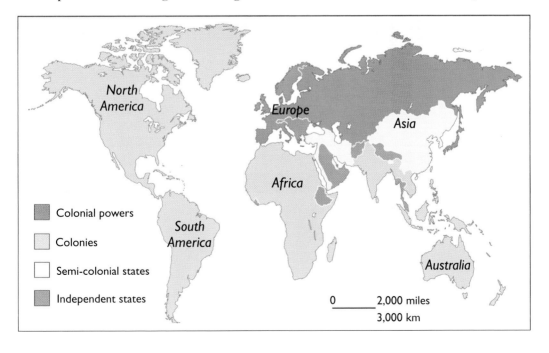

North America

Europe

Asia

Africa

South America

Australia

■ Colonial powers
☐ Colonies
☐ Semi-colonial states
▨ Independent states

0   2,000 miles
     3,000 km

Colonies and slaves

In the 1500s, European traders began to exploit countries in Africa, Asia, and South America for their precious metals, cloth, and crops. Later, they seized control of countries in Asia, Africa, South America, and the Caribbean to make it easier to use their resources. They governed the countries as colonies. The indigenous peoples of countries in South America and the Caribbean were mostly wiped out.

Areas such as North America, Australia, and New Zealand were occupied and settled by European colonizers, who then ruled those lands. Other countries, such as South Africa and Zimbabwe, were taken over and the native peoples were forced to work for their white rulers.

Because they had stronger military forces and could take over these countries, the Europeans believed they were better than nonwhites. They saw the colonized peoples as "children" who needed to be controlled. The Christian religion played an important role in this. The idea developed that Christian values were superior, and indigenous people were inferior because they were "pagans." This belief also helped to justify making people slaves.

During the 1600s, the slave trade developed. Iron goods, firearms, cloth, and brandy were brought from Europe and traded with African rulers in West Africa in exchange for slaves. Africans were bought and brutally transported in chains on overcrowded ships in disgusting conditions to the Americas. There they were forced to work on plantations for white owners, producing crops such as tobacco, cotton, and sugar to sell to Europe.

The Europeans tended to see Africans as "animals." They believed it was only right that these "animals" should work for them as beasts of burden. The Africans were black and the Europeans white. This led to a theory of racial difference between "superior" white masters and "inferior" black slaves.

African-American slaves pose on a farm in Maryland in 1862. Farm laborers—men, women, and children—did backbreaking work in the fields.

The 13th Amendment to the Constitution, supposedly ensuring equality for all American citizens, was passed in 1865, and the international slave trade was abolished in the 1880s. But black people still did not have equal rights in practice. In the United States, it was only when they fought for their rights in the 1960s that African Americans gained legal equality with white people. The legacy of slavery forms the historical background to racism in the United States and the rest of the American continent today.

Jewish inmates endure forced labor in a Nazi concentration camp in the 1940s. They are breaking up clay with picks. In addition to those not considered to be "pure" Germans, the Nazis sent their enemies, such as communists and trade unionists, to concentration camps.

Race hatred

It is January 1942. A group of Jewish people from Amsterdam in the Netherlands are ordered to meet at a train station. Each carrying a small bag of personal belongings, they are forced onto cattle trucks for a long, cold journey to a concentration camp. The very old, young, and weak are gassed to death on arrival. Nearly six million Jewish people and countless homosexuals, Romany Gypsies, and opponents of Nazism suffer the same fate. How did this horror come about?

During the 1920s and 1930s, Italy, Spain, and Germany came under the rule of fascist governments, each run by one extremely powerful dictator. The fascists believed their nation was superior to all others. They discriminated against minorities in their countries and used force to conquer other lands. The mass support for fascism came from the middle layer of society, from people who were neither rich nor poor. Many people running small businesses felt powerless, especially during times of economic crisis, and were attracted to the idea of a strong leader who would solve the country's problems.

Hitler and the "Master Race"

The most racist of the fascist powers was Nazi Germany. Its leader Adolf Hitler believed that Aryans (blue-eyed Germans and Scandinavians) were a superior "race." All other peoples, including Slavs and Africans, were useful only as slaves to this "master race." The worst enemy, he said, was Jewish people. He believed that Jewish people were inferior and that they were at the root of all of Germany's problems, destroying the country's economy from within.

In January 1942 at the height of World War II, senior Nazis met at the Wannsee Conference in

Berlin. They decided that all European Jews would be transported either to forced labor camps or to death camps in Poland, where they would be gassed to death. Valuable resources were diverted from the war effort for this murderous goal, and the European Jewish population was virtually destroyed.

Racism among the Allies

The countries fighting Germany were not immune from racism either. In the 1920s and 1930s, fascist movements in Britain and France carried out attacks on Jewish people and their property. But they were unable to achieve political power. After World War II, fascist ideas fell out of favor but did not die out completely. In recent times there has been an alarming increase in support for far-right parties in Europe.

In Britain in the 1930s, the British Union of Fascists (BUF), led by Oswald Mosley (second from the right), produced anti-Semitic propaganda and went on hostile demonstrations through Jewish areas of East London. BUF members were in favor of Nazi policies.

Separate and unequal

In the shanty town of Soweto, South Africa, in 1976, black children were squashed into an overcrowded classroom for their history lesson. The textbook described how the white people brought law and order to the barbarous tribes of South Africa. This is not the explanation they had heard from their parents, who had told them how 80 percent of the land was stolen by the white settlers. To add insult to injury, the children were then told they would have to study in Afrikaans, the language of their white rulers. This sparked the Soweto riots against white rule.

A badly wounded man is removed from the scene of disturbances during the Soweto riots of 1976. Students from Soweto had taken part in a demonstration against inferior education for black Africans. The police opened fire, and 176 people, mainly children and young people, were killed.

South Africa under apartheid is an example of a state run on racist ideas. The policy of apartheid ("apartness" in Afrikaans) was introduced by the National Party government in 1948. It made racial segregation official. All South Africans were classed as Bantu (black African), Colored (mixed race), White, or Asian. The Group Areas Act of 1950 established that each "race" had to live in a separate area, and nonwhites had to have a pass to be able to enter a white area. The different groups had separate schools and separate public facilities. Black people and white people could not mix at swimming pools or beaches or even use the same drinking fountain.

Apartheid kept people unequal. Black townships had rundown housing, badly equipped schools, and few doctors. Most white people had comfortable homes, top-quality schools, and excellent medical services.

The struggle against apartheid

There was always opposition to apartheid, including strikes against white employers, demonstrations, political campaigns, and guerrilla warfare. The South African police and army brutally stamped out resistance, imprisoning protesters and even murdering them. Yet opposition continued. One of the most significant anti-apartheid organizations was the African National Congress (ANC). Its leader, Nelson Mandela, was imprisoned in 1962.

The struggle continued and international support for the ANC grew. Some countries refused to trade with South Africa or to compete with South African athletes. Eventually President F. W. de Klerk was forced to negotiate. He released Mandela in 1990 and the apartheid regime was dismantled. The first free elections were held in 1994 and Nelson Mandela became the first black president of South Africa.

Protesters march against the apartheid government in Durban, South Africa, in 1989. By this time, the pressure on the apartheid regime was so great that it was clear it would soon have to give way to democracy.

DEBATE

Are all societies racist?

IMMIGRATION

Come to the motherland!

After World War II, European countries were short on labor. They sought workers from their colonies and former colonies. People in British colonies were granted British citizenship in 1948. They were given the right to live in Britain, and many were happy to go there. In the British West Indies (islands in the Atlantic Ocean between North and South America), for example, the cost of living had nearly doubled during the war, and there was widespread unemployment. No welfare benefits were available for the jobless and desperate.

These Kenyan immigrants arrived at Heathrow Airport, England, in 1968. Kenya had been a British colony, so they had the right to settle in Britain. However, they met with a high level of racism when they arrived.

By the mid-1960s, about a million immigrants from the West Indies, India, and Africa had come to Britain. Many of them found jobs in London Transport and the National Health Service doing vital work for the British economy. Many came as students, too. Yet when they arrived in the "motherland," they were in for a shock.

Half of Britain's population had never met a black person, but there was a lot of prejudice against them. More than two-thirds of the population disapproved of black people and held wild ideas about them. They thought they were ignorant and illiterate, wore few clothes, practiced black magic and head-hunting, ate strange food, and suffered from unpleasant diseases. Racism meant that black workers faced many difficulties. It was hard for them to find somewhere to live, and they were often paid lower wages than white workers.

Contributing to Europe's success

There was large-scale immigration to European countries, such as Germany and France, during this period, too. The largest group was Turks, followed by Algerians and Moroccans. People from southern European countries, such as Spain and Portugal, came, too. Some came as temporary workers, who stayed for a while to earn money for their families, while others settled permanently in Europe. These workers were essential to the success of Europe's industry. By the early 1970s, there were about eleven million migrant workers in Europe. One quarter of the industrial workforce in France, Belgium, and Switzerland was made up of immigrants. However, the European economies had begun to slow down. As unemployment and poverty rose in the early 1970s, immigrants were often blamed. Politicians responded by introducing immigration controls to restrict the flow of foreign workers.

VIEWPOINT

"No one knows exactly how the jobless live. It is not surprising that thousands have left the West Indies. The surprising thing is that so many have stayed."
Writer Joyce Egginton, 1957, describing the desperate poverty in the British West Indies after World War II

VIEWPOINT

"People look at me and assume I'm not an American. I still get compliments on the quality of my English. Often I hear, 'You speak English good.' My response is, 'You mean I speak English well.'"
Japanese American Dr. Roy Saigo, President of St Cloud State University, Minnesota

These Mexican agricultural workers are harvesting strawberries in Florida. Strawberries are too soft to pick using machines, so the work is done almost entirely by Mexican workers.

Seeking a better life

Large transnational corporations want to produce and distribute goods and services and invest money wherever they want, moving capital, workers, and goods as they please. This is economic globalization. Some say it makes producing goods cheaper, provides jobs, and creates wealth that trickles down through society. Yet the evidence shows that globalization has increased inequality in the world. Now, 85 percent of the world's population live in countries where the divide between rich and poor is growing. More and more people are forced to migrate to escape poverty.

In Mexico, Cuba, the Caribbean, and Central and South America, many people find it hard to find work. Daily life is a struggle. Many are attracted to the United States, where work is plentiful and wages are relatively high. Latin Americans,

including about 7 million Mexican Americans, make up 12.5 percent of the U.S. population. Despite their growing presence in society, Mexican Americans suffer from discrimination.

Stereotypes versus reality

Going to school is hard for newly arrived Latin-American children, because few schools offer education in both English and Spanish. For those who cannot speak good English, it is hard to get a decent job. In 2000 more than one in five Latin-American workers were in low-paid service jobs, compared to one in nine white workers. The media often portray young Latin Americans as school dropouts, involved in drugs and violence. People may say they are lazy, relying on welfare benefits. In fact most Latin Americans are very hardworking. Yet the stereotypes can lead to racism against Latin Americans.

Asian-Pacific Americans

Asian-Pacific Americans suffer from racism, too. Most were born in the United States, to families from China, Japan, Korea, India, the Philippines, and the Pacific Islands. The United States has fought many Asian countries in the past, during World War II, the Korean War, and the Vietnam War. Asians in the United States are sometimes still distrusted. They are often seen as foreigners who are not "real" Americans. One study showed that 25 percent of Americans had negative attitudes toward Chinese Americans.

FACT

In 2000, 80.4 percent of Latin-American men were in the U.S. workforce, compared to 74.3 percent of non-Latin-American men.

DEBATE

If companies can invest wherever they want, should workers also have the right to go wherever they want in order to work?

An Asian-American student (right) talks with a friend at the University of Texas at Austin. Many Asian Americans feel that white people lump all Asians together, without noticing the differences between different peoples, such as Chinese, Korean, Japanese, or Vietnamese.

Doing the dirty work

In general, immigrants do the jobs that local people do not want to do. For instance, many migrants come to southern Spain from North African countries such as Morocco. They work long hours in hot summer temperatures, picking fruits and vegetables on farms. These workers are generally not members of trade unions, and they accept worse pay and conditions than Spanish workers. In Saudi Arabia, there are thousands of workers from the Philippines. They have no rights at all. They are not even allowed to practice Christianity, because Islam is the only permitted religion.

Spanish police stopping a North African immigrant to inspect his documents. Moroccans have to have a visa to visit Spain. Yet farmers in southern Spain rely on Moroccan laborers, hired by the day, to pick their fruit and vegetables.

Because of the low-paying, manual jobs they tend to do, immigrants are often the target of racism. They are seen as inferior because of their occupations. When the economy is doing badly, far-right political parties blame immigrants for causing unemployment. They argue that immigrants are a burden on the economy, taking jobs away from local people.

Yet the truth is that an increase in the number of workers usually expands the economy. For example, during the 1960s and 1970s, there was a huge increase in the number of immigrant women working in the United States. This did not cause unemployment. In fact, a study in Los Angeles showed that the garment industry was able to survive only because of illegal Mexican immigrant workers. Without them, all the Americans working in the industry would have been out of a job.

Wanted: skilled workers

Projects have now been set up in countries, such as the United States, Germany, and Great Britain, to attract skilled foreign workers to areas where there are skill shortages. For instance, Indian computer programmers are welcomed in the United States. In 2001 the British government announced the introduction of a Highly Skilled Migrants Program, in order to encourage skilled workers such as doctors, information technology specialists, and scientists to migrate to Britain. These programs offer significant benefits for the host countries. The workers have been educated and trained at the cost of the country they come from. With a little training in the local way of doing things, they are soon ready to do the job.

VIEWPOINT

"I am a [lawyer] and I know that in many prisons around France at least 50 or 60 percent of the inmates are immigrants. What do these people do? They don't do any work."
Guy Macary, lawyer and National Front counselor, Carpentras, Provence, France.

VIEWPOINT

"Anyone who has had the misfortune to work ... flipping hamburgers, as a dishwasher in a hotel, or gutting chickens in rural factories knows the desperate scarcity of workers in jobs where the pay and conditions are rotten."
Nigel Harris, Professor of Urban Economics, University College London, Britain

Freedom of movement?

When people talk about problems with "immigrants," the word is usually a code word for "people of color." There are double standards when it comes to freedom of movement. White Europeans and Australians come freely to work in the United States and are typically accepted in workplaces without suffering racism. Nonwhite people, however, find it harder to enter the United States, even if they are married to an American. They meet with suspicion from the moment the flight touches down at the airport. At immigration controls, nonwhite people are more likely to be be stopped and questioned by officials. Some people believe that it is easier for white people of

This bar run by British people is in Fuengirola on the Costa del Sol in Spain, a popular destination for British tourists. People from within the European Union can live and work in any member country. White people find they are more easily accepted than black people, regardless of the country they come from.

European origin to integrate into the United States because they share the same culture. Yet each country has a mixture of cultures, so is this really the case? Or is it an example of racism?

If you are white and you come from inside the European Union, you can move anywhere in Europe without any difficulty. White British people can live in France or Spain for a while without being noticed. But black Europeans in Spain, for example, will arouse suspicion until it is clear that they are from a European Union member state. A question that sometimes runs through local people's minds is: "Has this person come to take my job?"

"Whites only"

Australia and Canada used to have a "whites only" immigration policy. In Australia this lasted from 1901 until 1966. Black people, Asian people, and those from Mediterranean countries were not allowed in. This has now changed, but the requirements for entering Australia are still strict. For example, in 2000–2001, the Australian government allowed in 40,000 skilled migrants with particular work skills and 34,400 close family members of Australian citizens or residents.

Despite these strict rules, there is still racism against nonwhite immigrants. In Australia, some fear that Asian immigrants are "flooding" the country. But the top countries of birth for people settling in Australia between 1993 and 1997 were New Zealand, Britain, and Ireland. In 1998–1999, a third of immigrants arrived from New Zealand and Britain. Some Australians believe that immigrants take local people's jobs even though they pay taxes, contribute savings from abroad, and spend money on food, housing, and services.

FACT

Four in ten Australians are migrants or the children of migrants.

DEBATE

Should people be able to live wherever they want in the world?

REFUGEES AND ASYLUM SEEKERS

Forced to flee conflict

Sometimes people have to leave their countries and seek refuge in another land. A few make the long journey to Western countries where they often experience racism. First, why do people have to leave their countries? Some examples will help to explain.

Rwanda and Afghanistan

In April 1994 there were mass killings in the Central African country of Rwanda due to a rivalry between the two main groups of people, the Hutu and the Tutsis. The conflict had its roots in colonial times when Belgian rulers encouraged differences between the two groups. After the Hutu president was assassinated, Hutu militias started killing both Tutsis and those Hutus who did not support the ruling party. About one million men, women, and children were hacked to death, burned alive, or shot in the massacre. Many refugees fled to nearby Tanzania and Burundi. When the Tutsi rebel forces took over the country, a million Hutu—both murderers and innocent bystanders—fled to Goma in the Democratic Republic of the Congo (Zaire). It was the fastest exodus of refugees in history.

Afghanistan has been in crisis since 1979 when the Soviet Union invaded. Over six million people left Afghanistan for Pakistan and Iran, and several hundred thousand Afghan professionals made their way to India, Europe, and North America. Many returned to Afghanistan, but there were further upheavals. First, the Soviet-backed government collapsed in 1992. Then, in 1994 an Islamic movement, the Taliban, began to fight with the already warring Mujahedin groups who were ruling the country. Throughout this unstable period, 3.5 million refugees stayed in neighboring Pakistan and Iran. In October 2001 the United States bombed Afghanistan in an attempt to root out the group that had carried out the terrorist atrocities on September 11. It was believed the attacks had been organized by Osama bin Laden, a terrorist leader living in Afghanistan. More people had to flee their homes or leave the country.

No choice but to leave

Most people are forced to become refugees because of conflict or natural disasters in the poorer countries of Africa and Asia. The vast majority go to neighboring countries that are also poor. It is a terrible thing to have to leave behind your home, land, and possessions. However, when the situation becomes extreme, some people have absolutely no choice.

FACT

In 1999 five African countries (Burundi, Democratic Republic of the Congo, Rwanda, Uganda, and Tanzania) took in a total of 1.2 million refugees. In the same year, Germany had 1,879,600 asylum applications, of which 7.6 percent (142,850) were recognized.

Afghan refugee children ride on a pickup truck loaded with all their belongings near the Pakistan-Afghan border in October 2001. This family made a dash for Pakistan, fearful of the U.S.-led bombing campaign to come. The Pakistani government soon closed its borders because it did not want more refugees to enter the country.

DEBATE

How can richer countries help poorer countries so that people are not forced to leave their homes as refugees?

Fleeing to escape persecution

In summer 2001 the body of a young Pakistani man named Mohammed Ayaz fell out of the undercarriage of a flying Boeing 777 into a parking lot in suburban Richmond, London. He had sprinted through the darkness of Bahrain Airport, in the Persian Gulf, and hauled himself up into the large opening above the wheels. He froze to death long before he reached British airspace. What makes a person so desperate that he is prepared to risk losing his life in such a terrifying manner?

Some people are forced to seek refuge in a distant country because they fear persecution in their homeland. They leave countries with political conflicts, such as Afghanistan, Algeria, Angola, Zimbabwe, the Democratic Republic of the Congo, and the former Yugoslavia. There are refugees from Zimbabwe who have campaigned against Robert Mugabe's government, which viciously crushes

Bosnian Muslim women and children gather for the first anniversary of the massacre of Srebrenica in 1995, when more than 7,000 Muslim men were murdered by Serbs because of their ethnicity.

opposition. People flee Algeria because of the political violence between the government and Islamic groups. Some people escape their country after they have been tortured or their families have been threatened with violence.

In search of asylum

Some refugees manage to reach Western countries and then have to go through an official process to seek asylum. Immigration officers in the host country check whether the applicant is really fleeing persecution. In Western countries today, some believe that many asylum seekers are "bogus." Rather than being genuine refugees, the view is that they are merely cheats who are trying to get to Europe or the United States through deceit.

Asylum seekers are often referred to as "flooding" European countries with a "tide" of foreigners. Yet the numbers tell a different story. For instance, in 2001, some 300,000 people left Britain, while a total of 200,000 entered the country.

Top Ten Nationalities of Asylum Applicants in the United States, Europe, Australia, and Canada in 2001	
In these countries, the problems include war, discrimination, political violence, and repression of opposition parties:	
Afghanistan	42,085
Iraq	41,238
Yugoslavia, Federal Republic	25,975
Turkey	27,515
China	18,712
Russia	17,795
India	12,929
Iran	12,205
Colombia	12,501
Bosnia and Herzegovina	11,010

Source: UNHCR, 2002

DEBATE

Should all asylum seekers be accepted wherever they go? Or is it fair to have quotas?

Settling in a new land

What happens to asylum seekers? In the United States, asylum seekers must apply for asylum within one year of arrival. The application takes up to 180 days to process, and applicants are not allowed to work during that time. Once people are granted asylum, they are expected to look for jobs and take an active part in integrating into the country. After one year, those granted asylum are finally allowed to apply for permanent resident status. People arriving in Australia without proper travel documents are placed in detention centers until their claims to asylum have been assessed. That can take months or even years.

In Britain asylum seekers are not allowed to work for six months while they are waiting to find out if the government is prepared to let them stay. They are given some money and usually housed in hostels or detention centers. Some argue that detention centers are a good idea. Asylum seekers can receive the services they need, such as interpreters and legal advisers, all in one place. They can also be protected against racist attacks. Yet asylum seekers who arrive at detention centers also have their fingerprints taken and have to carry special identity cards. Some argue that these measures mean that asylum seekers are treated like criminals.

Asylum seekers in Europe are often spread around the country to share the cost of caring for them among different communities. This can cause resentment among the local population and even cause racist attacks. People may blame asylum seekers for taking resources that should go to local people, even though the economic situation has nothing to do with the newcomers.

Asylum seekers from Sighthill Estate, on their way to hold a silent vigil in memory of Firsat Yildiz, turn their heads as local residents shout at them.

Murder of a migrant

Sighthill, in Glasgow, Scotland, is the housing development with the highest rate of male unemployment in Scotland. Many of the apartment buildings are empty. In April 2001 the local council decided to house nearly 2,000 asylum seekers there. The newcomers arrived, along with new equipment for the apartments. The situation was not explained to the existing residents. Some of them grew hostile to the asylum seekers, whom they saw as receiving special treatment. In August 2001, 22-year-old asylum seeker Firsat Yildiz, a Turkish Kurd, was brutally murdered. After this tragedy, efforts were finally made to build good relations between asylum seekers and local people.

DEBATE

Is it justifiable to lock up asylum seekers to make sure they do not disappear while their cases are being decided?

VIEWPOINTS

"Most asylum seekers are driven to Europe because of war and repression, rather than simply to seek greater wealth, according to a European Union report on forced migration."
Observer *newspaper, Great Britain, 2002*

"We resent the scroungers, beggars, and crooks who are prepared to cross every country in Europe to reach our generous benefits system."
Sun *newspaper, Britain, 2001*

Neo-Nazis, such as this group protesting in Germany in 1992, believe that asylum seekers should be sent back to their countries, no matter what they have endured there.

Bad press?

In Europe and Australia, asylum seekers have become targets of the press. Refugees are generally desperate people who have been forced to travel to a faraway land to seek refuge. Yet if much of what is written in the press can be believed, these lands are being "swamped" by a wave of "bogus" refugees who have come to take advantage of the welfare system and to live at the taxpayers' expense. This does not reflect the facts. In Britain, for example, asylum seekers receive only 70 percent of the amount British people receive as income support. They must survive at a level 30 percent below the poverty line.

A new stereotype of asylum seekers portrays them as criminals. A report by the UK Association of Chief Police Officers in 2001 showed that there was no evidence that refugees and asylum seekers committed more crimes than other people. In fact, they are more often the victims of crime and frequently suffer racist attacks.

However, the language used in the media fuels hatred of asylum seekers that can lead to prejudice against them. If local people are ignorant about refugees and asylum seekers, they may simply

believe what they read and adopt racist attitudes toward the newcomers. In Australia, for instance, a 2001 Equal Opportunity Commission report found significant racist stereotyping of asylum seekers, especially women. For example, Muslim women are often portrayed as weak and downtrodden. It has become acceptable in that society to treat them in a sexist manner.

Sister Abbas, a Muslim woman, teaches a kindergarten class in New Jersey. The idea that all Muslim women stay in the home and have no independent life is a stereotype.

The good news

Some attempts are being made to improve things. In Australia minority communities have worked with journalists on antiracist projects. The Australian-Arabic Council gives annual awards to Australian journalists who write positive stories that help to break down stereotypes of the Australian Arab community.

In all countries receiving asylum seekers, human rights organizations and refugee support groups constantly feed well-researched information about asylum seekers to the media. These help to counterbalance the wildly inaccurate tales that are all too frequently printed and broadcast.

DEBATE

Can articles in the press lead to violence on the streets?

INDIGENOUS PEOPLES IN A MODERN WORLD

The original peoples

All around the world, there are indigenous peoples who have had their land and rights taken away by colonists. Today they may legally have equal rights, yet they often suffer from racism. Their traditional lifestyle is often seen as "primitive."

Native Americans

In the United States, European settlers saw Native Americans as inferior. During the 1800s, the settlers took over nearly all of their land and wiped out the majority of Native Americans. The small numbers who survived were forced to move to reservations, usually areas of poor, infertile land, far from their original homelands.

For example, the Cherokee of the southern United States had to move west when gold was discovered in their territory. In 1838 they were marched to Oklahoma. One in four died from cold, hunger, or disease. The march became known as the "Trail of Tears." A few hundred Cherokee escaped and were later given a small reservation in North Carolina.

Today, there are only about three million Native Americans in the United States and Canada. Some groups continue to speak their own language and follow a traditional lifestyle, but more than half of all Native Americans live in cities, away from their own communities.

This Native American man makes a living by selling traditional handicrafts to tourists. Native Americans are some of the poorest people in North American society. In 1999 26 percent of them lived in poverty, compared to 12 percent of the general population.

Certain groups have adapted aspects of their culture to help them survive, for example, selling pottery and traditional handicrafts to tourists. However, most face poverty, unemployment, and racism. They are often still seen as inferior and put under pressure to integrate into mainstream society.

The Maya

The Maya are the original inhabitants of Guatemala, who were virtually wiped out by the Spanish colonists of the 1500s. Today they are "at the bottom of the heap" in a society that is divided along racial lines (despite the 1985 constitution, which forbids discrimination). In the 1980s, around 20,000 Maya were killed by the Guatemalan army during a civil war over land ownership and human rights.

The Maya suffer from institutional racism. The way society is organized puts them at a great disadvantage. Most live in poverty in rural areas, where there is a lack of health care and schools. Less than half the population has access to running water. The main problem is land. Most Maya have no land or not enough to support themselves.

VIEWPOINT

"Our rights have always been violated. We Maya are not respected as a people; we are ignored; we have few opportunities."
Minority Rights Group seminar report, "Views and Proposals of the Maya people of Guatemala," 1994

FACT

In 2001 infectious diseases were twelve times more common among indigenous people in Australia than among the rest of the population.

Aborigine children perform a welcome Corroboree dance at Broken Hill to mark the launch of the 2002 tourism campaign, "The Year of the Outback." There has been a revival of interest in Aborigine culture and some indigenous people are able to make a living from their arts, crafts, music, and dance.

The Aborigines of Australia

Indigenous peoples in countries taken over by settlers were not allowed to continue their traditional lifestyles undisturbed. After the British landed in Australia in 1788, they occupied the land. Most of the native Aborigines were killed, leaving a few in desolate areas. The Europeans held racist views about the Aborigines. They considered them to be animals rather than people, which in their minds justified seizing their land.

From the early 1800s onward, indigenous children were taken from their families to work for settlers. The government decided that it was better for Aborigine children to be brought up by "civilized" white people. These forced removals continued until the 1970s. Since then, many people who were taken from their families have tried to find their real

parents. The process of reuniting families after decades of painful separation still continues.

In Australia today, there is a legacy of institutional racism. Aborigines experience the lowest standards of health, education, employment, and housing. In 1998 only 32 percent of Aborigine children completed schooling, compared with 73 percent of all Australian youth. An Aborigine is more likely to be sent to prison than a white person who has committed the same crime. The imprisonment rate for indigenous peoples in 1997 was over fourteen times that for nonindigenous adults. Racism is a major factor to this statistic.

Some positive steps have been taken. Since the Native Title Act, which came into being in 1994, Aborigines have been able to reclaim some of the land they lost to white settlers. There is now a renewed pride in Aborigine culture. There is still a long way to go, however, to achieve equality.

The Inuit

The Inuit are a native people in Canada. Throughout the 20th century, they were put under pressure by the government to leave their traditional hunting life and settle in villages. Many Western environmental groups attacked their tradition of hunting seals and whales without understanding how the Inuit took no more of these animals than they needed to live. Inuit children were sent to boarding schools and the whole culture was threatened.

In 1999, the Inuit achieved self-government in their own province in the Northwest Territories called Nunavut. Nunavut represents a victory for a native people, an independent province where Inuit culture is dominant. The Inuit have gained land rights here, and the right to hunt wildlife.

FACT

According to a 1997 report, between 10 and 30 percent of Australian Aborigine children were forced to leave their families and communities between 1910 and 1970.

VIEWPOINTS

"The transition from a traditional ... society which only a generation ago was nomadic, entails relinquishing [giving up] values, customs, and a traditional economy."
Dr. Ben-David, Jerusalem Institute of Israel Studies, Israel

"These Bedouin are citizens of the Jewish state, but aside from a passport and a right to vote, there are few other benefits that [have] found their way to these shanty towns."
Chris Doyle, Council for Arab-British Understanding

Racism against nomads

People who live their lives on the move, such as the Roma of eastern Europe and the Batwa of the Great Lakes in Africa, are often targets of racism. The settled population tends to distrust "outsiders" who enter their neighborhoods. It is common to believe that travelers are criminals, and they are frequently suspected of stealing.

The Bedouin

The word *Bedouin* means "inhabitant of the desert." It refers to the desert-dwelling nomads of Arabia, the Negev, and the Sinai. Since the 1300s Bedouin groups used to travel by camel from oasis to oasis through the desert, following a traditional nomadic way of life. An area of desert could support life for only a short time, so the Bedouin, with their herds of sheep and goats, would regularly migrate to new areas.

A Bedouin shepherd walks with his flock in the hills near Bethlehem in the West Bank.

Many Bedouin have exchanged their traditional way of life for a settled existence. This process of change has been especially marked over the last two decades. Bedouin culture still survives in the Sinai desert in particular, but it is declining in Israel.

Within Israel there are about 170,000 Bedouin. Approximately 110,000 of them live in the Negev desert, the majority in settled communities. There are different views on this.

A girl hangs up laundry beside her family's tin shacks in a Bedouin community outside the town of Haifa, northern Israel. The Bedouin have traditionally lived in rural areas but now they are often drawn toward towns, where there are more jobs.

The Israeli government sees settlement as progress, an opportunity for the Bedouin to integrate into Israeli society. For example, by law all Bedouin children have to go to school. As a result, the literacy rate for Bedouin has improved from 25 percent to 95 percent in one generation. There are clinics in all the Bedouin towns and most women now give birth in hospitals rather than at home.

However, many Bedouin feel they suffer discrimination. Despite being Israeli citizens with the right to vote, they are not provided the same level of services as Israeli Jews. For instance, it is hard for the Bedouin to get a permit to build on the land. Half of the Bedouin in the Negev desert live in badly equipped shanty towns that are not legally recognized by the Israeli government. Services for their settlements, such as roads, transport, and communications, are poor. The Bedouin feel neglected and deprived.

DEBATE

Should the Bedouin have the right to decide to continue to live in a traditional way, or is it the responsibility of governments to integrate them into modern society?

ETHNIC MINORITIES

Cultural differences

An ethnic minority is a group of people who share a common culture, tradition, and sometimes language. Most countries have ethnic minorities, and racism is frequently directed against them because they are seen as being "different." For example, Koreans in Japan are seen as outsiders and often treated badly, even though their families may have lived in Japan for decades. Western racists nowadays tend to say their problems with ethnic minorities are due to "cultural differences." These may be linked to religious differences.

Religious racism

Sikhs are proud of their culture. Male members of the religion wear a turban on their heads. This is to cover their uncut hair and keep it tidy. Uncut hair is one of the five symbols of Sikhism worn by believers. Sikhs may suffer racism, because the turban makes them look different.

In February 2000, Sikh students at a school in a small community near Toronto, Canada, were attacked in a snowball fight that turned to name-calling, slapping, and racist insults. Two non-Sikhs who tried to stop the abuse were also attacked. At one point, a turban was ripped off the head of one of the students and hurled into a trash can. This was an openly racist attack.

Islamophobia

Some people in Western countries argue that Islamic traditions are at odds with their traditions, which makes it hard to integrate Muslims into

Western society. This has developed into a fear of Islam in the United States and Europe, known as *Islamophobia*. Certain stereotypes are spread about Muslims; for example, that they are cruel to animals because of the way they slaughter them for food. They are accused of treating women unfairly, of supporting terrorism, of being very extreme in their religious views, and of not favoring the democratic way of life.

These stereotypes have been taken up by far-right parties in the United States as a way of singling out Muslims as outsiders who should not be welcomed. This is thinly veiled racism. The Muslim community, like other groups, includes a huge variety of shades of opinion and lifestyle. And all countries are made up of a mixture of cultures.

VIEWPOINT

"Research published in the *British Medical Journal* tested racism in the medical profession by sending out applications for jobs in a variety of specialties, half with an Asian name and half with an English-sounding name. The Asian names were far less likely to be shortlisted."
Polly Toynbee, writing in the Guardian *newspaper, Britain, 2000*

DEBATE

Is it harder for people from certain cultures to integrate into Western countries?

Muslims worship at a mosque in Philadelphia, Pennsylvania. Non-Muslims often believe that Muslims put their religion before their country, and therefore cannot be trusted. Many see Islam as an intolerant religion, but actually they themselves are being intolerant of people who are different.

The World Trade Center and after

The terrorist attacks on the twin towers of the World Trade Center in New York and the Pentagon in Washington D.C., on September 11, 2001 were condemned throughout the world. These atrocities were almost certainly carried out by a group of radical Muslims with extreme anti-American views.

Muslims from a New York mosque march to show support for the United States, following the terrorist attacks of September 11, 2001.

However, many people in the United States and elsewhere blamed the attacks on Muslims in general, even though most Muslims were just as outraged as non-Muslims. This led to attacks on Muslim communities and a general rise in racism.

At a peace rally in New York immediately after the attacks, a young Muslim woman described how she was too frightened to go shopping for groceries. She knew that people of Arab appearance were being physically attacked in the streets of her neighborhood.

Not only Muslims suffered; many others in the United States and Europe were attacked for "looking Arab" or "being of Middle Eastern appearance." In October 2001, it was reported that two Sikhs were beaten to death in Seattle, Washington. A gunman drove into a garage in Phoenix, Arizona, and shot dead the Sikh owner. The prejudiced people who carried out these attacks mistook their victims for Muslims. They thought they looked like members of the Taliban forces in Afghanistan.

Under suspicion

Official discrimination also occurred. For instance, in October 2001, twelve Sikhs were forced off an airplane in the United States after being informed that they were not permitted to travel unless they removed their turbans. The U.S. security services took in people of "Middle Eastern appearance" for questioning, even including some Israelis. (Israel is a country closely allied to the United States.)

In Germany, after September 11, the police began to comb the country in search of Islamic "extremists." There are some 3.5 million Muslims in Germany. The Head of the Council of Muslims, Nadeem Elyas, complained that many innocent Muslims were being arrested. Then in February 2002, it was announced that all Muslim men aged twenty to forty would be called in by the police for questioning. This abuse of human rights was deemed necessary because of the possible danger to society from terrorist attacks.

VIEWPOINT

"When Muhammad Ali, the boxing champ, visited the attack site at the World Trade Center, a reporter asked him, 'How do you feel about the suspected hijackers sharing your faith?' Ali answered, 'How do you feel about Hitler sharing yours?'"
Seattle Post-Intelligencer, October 2001

DEBATE

Is it right for the police to arrest or question people on the basis of their religion alone? Will this kind of precaution really protect the population against the risk of future attack?

VIEWPOINT

"You name the problem, the disease, the human suffering, or the abject misery visited upon millions, and I'll bet you ten bucks I can put a white face on it.... And yet when I turn on the news each night, what do I see again and again? Black men alleged to be killing, raping, mugging...."
U.S. filmmaker and writer Michael Moore, Stupid White Men, 2002

Scapegoating

A young Roma in Romania is accused by racist skinheads of stealing. He is taken in by the police for questioning. They beat him up at the police station. He notices that one of the police officers was one of the skinheads.

When a group of people is wrongly accused of causing problems, such as committing crime, they are being made into scapegoats. For example, since the fall of communism in Eastern Europe after 1989, the economies of the region have collapsed. The rise in unemployment has been accompanied by a decline in welfare services provided by the state to help needy people. A small minority of people have achieved wealth, while poverty in general has risen. In this situation, victims of economic crisis may blame others around them—often people from ethnic minorities—rather than their government.

The Roma are travelers who originally left India in about the 10th century and have always migrated to different countries. There are large Roma communities in eastern European countries, especially Romania, Bulgaria, Hungary, and Slovakia. The Roma have always been scapegoated by people in settled communities, who often distrust them and blame them for crime. Racist attacks against Roma are frequent, and local people usually try to keep them out of their communities.

Roma children in front of their apartment block in the city of Plovdiv, Bulgaria. The Roma suffer discrimination in education, housing, and employment, and sometimes endure vicious racist attacks by other Bulgarians.

The Chinese in Indonesia

In Indonesia the ethnic Chinese are scapegoats. Resentment of the Chinese dates back to colonial times, when the Dutch rulers allowed the Chinese to be traders while locals were used as plantation slaves. A section of the Chinese community came to dominate economic life. Yet the Indonesian state has never accepted the Chinese as full citizens. They are not officially allowed to be involved in politics or join the military or civil service.

During the deep political and economic crisis that led to the resignation of Indonesia's dictator, Suharto, in 1998, the Chinese were blamed for the collapse of the economy. Mobs of armed young men chanting anti-Chinese slogans killed at least 2,000 ethnic Chinese during riots in the capital, Jakarta. Unfortunately, a government in crisis may sometimes be content for people to blame an ethnic minority rather than its own failings.

VIEWPOINT

"They [the Chinese] have become parasites."
Indonesian politician and former presidential candidate, Amien Rais, quoted in Asiaweek *magazine, 1998*

Indonesian rioters burn items they have seized from Chinese shops in Jakarta during the riots of 1998.

FACT

In the United States, three out of four drug users are white. However, African Americans are more likely to be arrested and usually receive longer prison sentences than white people.

The Kurds

In 2001 the Turkish government was planning to drown the ancient city of Hasankeyf in Anatolia, Turkey, in order to build the giant Ilisu Dam. This would have destroyed the homes of 78,000 Kurdish people. A campaign by their supporters defeated the plan, but the Kurds' plight remains desperate.

Cattle drink from the Tigris River, with the ancient city of Hasankeyf in the background. To the Turkish government, building a dam to provide hydroelectric power seemed more important than preserving the homes and livelihoods of the Kurdish people of Hasankeyf.

A minority living mostly in Turkey, Iraq, Syria, and Iran, the Kurds want their own independent homeland, Kurdistan. They have suffered horrendous persecution. In Iraq thousands of Kurds died and many more lost their homes during the Iran-Iraq war (1980–1988). They were persecuted after the Gulf War (1991) and have been used to test the effects of Iraqi chemical and biological weapons.

In Turkey the state takes the racist view that the Kurds do not exist as a people. Kurdish music, history, celebrations, and language are all banned. The Kurds have suffered terribly for defying this repression; whole villages have been destroyed and thousands murdered.

The Palestinians

The Palestinians are also trying to gain a homeland. In 1947 Jewish settlers in Palestine owned 7 percent of the land. During war with the Arab states in 1948, they captured up to three-quarters of the land as the Palestinians fled. Most of the remaining territory, the West Bank and Gaza Strip, is now also occupied by Israel. Israel is a Jewish state that allows any Jewish person to become a citizen, while Palestinian refugees are not allowed to return.

The legal system in the West Bank and Gaza Strip separates Israelis from Palestinians. Israeli settlers have seized much of the land, taken control of water resources, and built roads. In 2002 the Gaza Strip, the most densely populated area in the world, held 1.1 million Palestinians. Most of them were living in tiny shacks in dusty refugee camps. The 7,000 Israeli settlers inhabited 25 settlements, living in houses surrounded by crops.

The Palestinians feel the Israeli state is racist and they have always struggled against Israeli rule. Many Israelis feel that Palestinians are racist toward Jewish people, and fear terrorist attacks. The most recent *intifada*, or uprising, began in 2000. Palestinian suicide bombers entered Israel and blew themselves up in public places, killing Israeli citizens. The Israeli forces attacked Palestinian areas where they believed bombers were being sheltered and trained. Between September 2000 and August 2002, over 1,370 Palestinians and more than 150 Israeli civilians were killed. No end to the conflict is in sight.

FACT

When the state of Israel was established in 1948, war with nearby Arab states immediately followed. As a result of this war, millions of Palestinians were displaced to neighboring Arab countries. They have been trying to establish their own homeland ever since.

DEBATE

Should every ethnic minority be allowed to form a homeland if the majority of its people wish to?

NATIONALISM AND NEO-FASCISM

Divide and rule in India

In February 2002, a Muslim crowd burned alive 58 Hindu nationalist activists on a train in Gujarat, India. This led to riots in which Hindus killed more than 600 Muslims.

Nationalism can mean taking pride in your country, its culture, history, and people. Extreme nationalists, though, may feel that their ethnic group alone has the right to live in their country, and that others are unwelcome outsiders. Although India is a country with both Muslim and Hindu traditions, divisions between Hindus and Muslims deepened under British colonial rule (1858–1947) and remained after India became independent.

Muslims in Pakistan burn an effigy in protest against the Indian government for failing to prevent 600 Muslims from being killed in Gujarat by Hindu militants. Extreme Hindu nationalism is very strong in India and many Muslims fear for their future.

The violence in 2002 came about because of the rise of Hindu nationalism. The nationalist party, the BJP, runs the Indian government. Many of its supporters hold strongly racist views against Muslims, who make up 11 percent of the population. They want to build a pure and patriotic Hindu state. These nationalists see the Muslims as "terrorists" and cruel people, who should be kept in an inferior position in society. At the heart of the conflict is the plan to build a Hindu temple on the ruins of the Muslims' Ayodhya mosque, which was destroyed by Hindu militants in 1992. If the nationalists get their way and the Hindu temple is built, India could become a country where mosques are destroyed and racism against Muslims is the norm.

Ethnic cleansing in the former Yugoslavia

Between 1991 and 1999 in the former Yugoslavia, about 150,000 people were killed, three million were displaced, and countless thousands were raped, tortured, and imprisoned. The Serb leader, Slobodan Milosevic, masterminded a policy of "ethnic cleansing." By expelling non-Serbs, he tried to carve out a purely Serb country, "Greater Serbia," from the ruins of Yugoslavia.

In February 2002 Milosevic was put on trial by the United Nations for war crimes. He was charged with expelling 800,000 Kosovan Albanians and 170,000 Croats and non-Serbs, and the murder of hundreds of other people. He was also accused of being responsible for the Srebrenica massacre in 1995 in which about 7,000 Bosnian Muslims were murdered. Ethnic cleansing can be seen as a form of racism. It involves expelling people simply because they are not from the ethnic group in power.

VIEWPOINTS

"Man, I am scared of these [Muslims]. We are a secular, modern nation, but we let them run these madrasas [religious schools], we let them breed like rabbits, and one day they are going to outstrip the Hindu population, and will they then treat us as well as we treat them?"
Hindu nationalist in Benares, India

"We expect nothing from the government and political parties. We now depend on the good will of the Hindus we live with, and all that we hope for is survival with a bit of dignity."
Najam, a Muslim from Benares

DEBATE

Can any country ever be "purely" of one ethnic group? Would this be a good thing anyway?

Jean-Marie Le Pen speaks at a National Front conference in France in 2002. The National Front, a political party in France since 1972, did not have a big impact at a national level until 2002. The large vote for Le Pen in the first round of the presidential elections in April 2002 was a shock to antiracists.

The Hitlers of today?

When Hitler came to power in 1933, many people did not imagine that he would create a vicious, dictatorial regime that murdered Jewish people and Nazi opponents in the millions. Today there is no such excuse. Yet in Europe today, neo-fascist parties, with policies based on Hitler's ideas, are campaigning for political power.

During the 1990s, right-wing parties gained ground in Europe. By 2002 fascist organizations had gained some degree of political power in Austria, Belgium, France, Holland, Denmark, Italy, and Portugal. Fascist parties feed on people's disappointment with the failure of left-wing governments to improve life for ordinary people. They claim they are concerned about the issues that worry the majority of people, including the decline in the provision of services such as education, health, and housing. Yet they scapegoat immigrants and asylum seekers rather than addressing the roots of these problems.

Jean-Marie Le Pen, leader of the National Front in France, has been described by many as a Nazi. In 1987 he said the murder of 6 million Jews in the Holocaust was a mere "detail of history." In April 2002, Le Pen won 17 percent of the vote in the first round of the French presidential elections, pushing the left-wing Prime Minister Lionel Jospin into third place. Although Le Pen was defeated in the second round of the elections, the fact remained that 6 million people had voted for him.

The far-right in Holland

In Holland right-wing politician Pim Fortuyn, leader of the List Pim Fortuyn Party, opposed immigration, arguing that Holland was "full." In fact, Holland has a rapidly falling birth rate and a growing elderly population, and needs immigrant labor. Fortuyn disguised his racism using the language of cultural differences. He argued for a "vital and aggressive Dutch culture" to oppose the "threat of Islam." Fortuyn claimed Islam was a "backward culture" that was unfair to women and discriminated against homosexuals. He was murdered shortly before the elections of May 2002 and his party gained 18 percent of the vote.

It seems that many Europeans have lost faith in the ability of mainstream political parties to solve society's problems. Some are prepared to look to the fascist right, despite its frightening legacy.

Right-wing marchers gather for a demonstration in France in 1988.

VIEWPOINT

"There's no difference between the program of the socialist[s] or of Chirac's [the center right] party. They have swapped power for 20 years, and we have had no real change. This support for Le Pen is not a question of extremism or fascism; it's despair."
Thierry d'Egremont, a Frenchman who voted for Le Pen

Extremists in the United States

In 1995 a bomb explosion in Oklahoma City, Oklahoma, ripped apart a federal office building, killing 169 people and injuring 500. The bomber, Timothy McVeigh, was linked to a far-right organization.

The United States is home to many hate organizations, most of which are racist. The oldest and best known is the Ku Klux Klan (KKK), which has a violent history of torture, murder, and bombings of African Americans. Since the 1970s, it has been greatly weakened. Today, some KKK groups are still openly racist and violent. Others try

A Ku Klux Klan member speaks during a rally in Jasper, Texas. It is estimated that there were about 6,000 Klan members in 2001, divided among many different and often warring groups.

to hide their racism by saying they are in favor of "civil rights for whites," rather than opposed to African Americans or other groups. They appear to feel threatened by the diverse culture of the United States, which has been created by people of many different nationalities.

Neo-Nazis

Members of neo-Nazi groups, such as the National Alliance in the United States, hate Jewish people and admire the policies of Adolf Hitler's government in Nazi Germany. They believe there is a worldwide Jewish conspiracy to control the world. Some of these groups focus on hatred, while others aim to create a fascist state. American neo-Nazi groups are protected by the First Amendment, a law that gives them the right to free speech. They can produce publicity and host Internet sites containing material that would be illegal under antiracist laws in Europe. Because of this, many European neo-Nazi groups register their sites with American servers to avoid being prosecuted under the laws of their own country.

The message of hatred

The Internet is also used to distribute "white power" rock music, with its racist lyrics. Racists are able to spread their message of hatred more effectively online. This message does not come from white groups alone. Some African Americans today argue for black separatism. They believe that the only solution to racism is for black people to separate from white society. Their hatred of other groups is almost certainly a response to the racism they have suffered themselves. However, the views of some groups are themselves racist. For example, members of the biggest black separatist organization, the Nation of Islam, have expressed strongly anti-Semitic opinions. They scapegoat Jewish people for the problems in U.S. society.

FACT

In the United States in 2001, there were 209 neo-Nazi groups, 109 KKK groups, 51 African-American separatist groups, and 43 racist skinhead groups.

DEBATE

Should neo-fascists have the right to freedom of speech? Or should their organizations and websites be closed down? If racist organizations are banned, will they become more secretive and harder to keep an eye on?

WHAT CAN BE DONE TO FIGHT RACISM?

A U.S. soldier escorts an African-American student to the formerly all-white Little Rock High School, Arkansas, in 1957. Many white people were angered by the decision to allow African-American students to attend, and the children had to be protected.

Using the law

Wherever there has been racism, people have struggled against it. Sometimes these struggles have brought about dramatic changes that have improved the lives of millions. For example, in the South as late as the 1950s, African Americans had to use separate public facilities from whites. They attended separate, inferior schools, and they had to sit in different parts of buses, libraries, and movie theaters from whites. In the mid-1950s, African Americans formed organizations to campaign for equal rights. Many white people also became involved in the fight for justice. Marches, demonstrations, and petitions were organized. Eventually in 1964, the Civil Rights Act was passed, making it illegal for public institutions such as schools to discriminate against African Americans.

More recently in South Africa, massive pressure led to the end of the apartheid regime. In 1990 the legal system was changed to give every person an equal vote, enabling black South Africans to vote for the national government for the first time. In Australia the law was changed in 1994 to allow Aborigines to begin to reclaim land taken from them by white settlers long ago.

Tackling institutional racism

Laws against racism are essential. However, to really tackle the problem of racism in society, institutions and individuals need to change, too. For example, in 1993 the murder of black teenager Stephen Lawrence sent shockwaves around Great Britain. The police had information about a gang of knife-carrying racists who had boasted about attacking black people. Yet none of these suspects was immediately arrested. Stephen's parents, Neville and Doreen Lawrence, kept up pressure on the police to find their son's killers.

Doreen and Neville Lawrence, the parents of the murdered teenager, Stephen Lawrence. In 2002 two of the young men believed by many to have killed him were arrested for another race-hate crime. They were never charged with Stephen's murder.

In 1998 a government inquiry into the case revealed institutional racism in the police force. It showed that the police had failed to provide adequate service in the hunt for Stephen's killers because the Lawrences were black. In fact the British police themselves have been responsible for killing black people in their charge—140 of them between 1969 and 2002. This indicates that there is still a lot to be done to solve police racism.

Out on the streets

After extreme-right leader Le Pen came in second in the first round of the French presidential elections in April 2002, tens of thousands of people, young, old, black, Arab, and white, poured into the streets of France to protest. Many wept tears of shock. They hoped this was the start of a huge campaign to drive Le Pen and his far-right followers out of French politics. His party, the National Front, did not win a single seat in the parliamentary elections in June 2002.

A huge demonstration took place in Paris on May 1, 2002 to protest against Le Pen and his racist politics.

Antiracist organizations exist around the globe to counter racism. They take part in a wide range of activities, from holding debates, to painting over racist graffiti, leafleting, petitioning, and demonstrating. If ethnic minorities are targeted by far-right groups, antiracist organizations come forward to defend them.

In the United States and Canada, Anti-Racist Action (ARA) groups have been formed in cities such as Chicago, Toronto, and Los Angeles. They have set up phone lines for people to report racist incidents and organized *Rock Against Racism* benefit concerts, posters, and educational materials.

Youth against Racism in Europe (YRE), formed in 1992, brings together young people to oppose racism in fifteen European countries. It played an important role in the campaign to shut down the headquarters of the fascist British National Party in Kent, Britain, in 1993. YRE also fights racism in soccer. The group produces a magazine called *Show Racism the Red Card* and campaigns to stop racist thugs at soccer matches from abusing black and Asian players and fans.

In 1986 an organization called Pro Asyl was set up in Germany to defend asylum seekers. In 1992–1993, which was a period of vicious racist attacks against refugees living in hostels, Pro Asyl launched a mass media campaign and called for demonstrations to defend refugees.

The Anti-Nazi League (ANL) was reestablished in Britain in 1992 because of the rise of neo-fascism in Europe. The ANL says that parties such as the British National Party (BNP) and the National Front in France are not merely far-right parties. They are made up of Nazis, says the ANL, who wish to repeat the events of the Holocaust. The ANL opposes Nazi activities through anti-Nazi propaganda and protests. Given the rise of the extremist right today, the ANL and other antiracist organizations have much work to do.

VIEWPOINT

"After you heard the result [Le Pen's 17 percent vote in April 2002] you wanted to cry. But then you felt you had to do something about what had happened."
Fabrice, a student on a march against Le Pen, France, 2002

VIEWPOINTS

"Wherever Nazis in Britain try to organize, they need to be opposed and their ideas exposed for what they are."
Paul Holborow, Peter Hain, member of Parlaiment, and Ernie Roberts, ANL, Britain, 1992

"We're sweeping across Europe.... It [the far right] could be here next."
Mark Collett, BNP candidate in British local elections, 2002

Education, education, education

A lack of understanding between different ethnic groups can lead to racism. Education is vital in order to bridge the gap. If children learn about the history and culture of the various ethnic groups in their society, they can develop respect for them. This helps to break down the barriers of ignorance and decrease racism.

Actress Halle Berry speaks at the ceremony in 2002 where she won an Oscar for her performance in the film Monster's Ball.

Individuals can make a difference, too. It is important for people to speak out if they hear racist jokes or witness bullying. School teachers and students can develop policies against racism. This will all help to develop a positive, antiracist atmosphere at school.

In Australia a 2001 report revealed that Aborigines felt the lack of teaching about their history was a kind of racism in itself. It was agreed that teaching the history of indigenous peoples from their point of view and avoiding stereotypes was the way forward. But learning does not just happen in schools. It was recognized that public education campaigns were also needed to get the antiracist message across to society at large.

Media representation for minorities

In 2002 the film world was astonished when African-American film stars Denzel Washington and Halle Berry were awarded Oscars for best actor and best actress. Some hoped this was a sign of change, a breakthrough for African Americans in an industry traditionally dominated by white faces.

Yet in the United States, most African-American and Hispanic actors work on programs aimed at those minority audiences. In Britain, there are 200 black and Asian newspapers and magazines but few black or Asian journalists working on national newspapers. If there were more people from ethnic minorities working in the media, they could help to counter racist stereotypes.

The future
Will racism always exist? Many believe that the division between rich and poor is likely to increase between and within nations. Growing poverty may lead to more people feeling the anger and hopelessness that can in turn cause scapegoating and racism. Providing people with a decent standard of living would lessen those feelings. Racism causes division, distrust, hatred, and pain. Celebrating and enjoying the vibrant mix of cultures that exists in many countries around the world can only enrich our lives.

FACT

In the mid-to-late 1990s, in a workforce of some 3,000 journalists working on national newspapers in Britain, only 20 were black.

DEBATE

What do you believe is the most effective method of stopping racism—the law, antiracist campaigns, or education?

A crowd cheers at the Notting Hill Carnival in London, a huge multicultural event. Enjoying aspects of different cultures can help to break down barriers of ignorance and fear. Even in areas where there are few people from ethnic minorities, it is vital to learn about the different groups that contribute to society.

GLOSSARY

anthropologist someone who studies humans, especially their origins

anti-Semite one who hates Jewish people

apartheid meaning "apartness," a system of government introduced in South Africa in 1948 to keep black, white, mixed-race, and Asian people separate and unequal

asylum seeker someone who suffers because of his or her skin color, culture, religion, or political beliefs and flees to another country to seek asylum, a safe haven. Asylum is the right to live in another country if you have been attacked for one of these reasons.

bogus false; not genuine

colonies lands ruled by another country, as if owned by it

concentration camp a type of prison where political prisoners are kept in extremely bad conditions. The Nazis set up some concentration camps as death camps where millions were deliberately murdered in gas chambers.

detention center a secure area, like a prison, where people who have entered a country illegally have to stay until it is decided whether they will be allowed to stay in the country

discrimination treating a group of people worse than other groups

ethnic cleansing the policy of forcing the people of a particular ethnic group or religion to leave an area or country

ethnic group a group of people who share a common culture, tradition, and sometimes language

European Community/European Union an organization of mostly Western European countries committed to economic and political integration. It came into being in 1967, and in 2002 there were fifteen member countries.

fascist someone who believes that his or her country or ethnic group is better than all others, obeys one powerful leader, and opposes democracy

globalization the free operation of businesses all around the world, investing anywhere, trading in any types of goods and services, and employing labor anywhere

guerrilla warfare war waged by a small group of soldiers, who are not part of an official army, against a regular army

Hispanic someone from a Latin American country living in the United States

homeland the country where a person was born

immigrant a person who goes to live permanently in another country

immigration controls laws to control the number of immigrants that are permitted to enter a country

indigenous people people who have lived in a country from the very earliest times, such as the Native Americans in the United States, Aborigines in Australia, and the Maya in Guatemala

institutional racism racism entrenched in the way society is organized, from housing to the education system and the job market, resulting in particular groups being treated unfairly

Islamophobia fear of Islam and of Muslim people

migrant someone who moves from one country or region to another

militant a person who is aggressively active, usually in support of a political cause

militia a group of people who are not professional soldiers but have had military training and act as an army

Mujahedin Islamic guerrilla fighters who aim to set up an Islamic state, as in Afghanistan in 1992

Nation of Islam an African-American organization in the United States. Its members fight for black people's rights and believe that they should run their own organizations, separate from white society.

National Front the French far-right political party led by Jean-Marie Le Pen

nationalism a sense of pride in their country felt by many people. Extreme nationalists may believe that only their own ethnic group should have the right to live in their country.

persecution treating someone badly, often on the grounds of their ethnic group or culture or their religious or political beliefs

prejudice negative feelings toward a group of people that are not based on factual information

quota the number of immigrants or refugees that are allowed to enter a country

repress to use political or military force to control a group of people and restrict their freedom

Roma a traveling people, with their own language and culture, who live mostly in eastern Europe

scapegoat to blame a certain group of people for a problem in society, such as unemployment or poor housing, that is not their fault

segregation the policy of keeping different groups of people apart, often on the basis of their ethnic group

separatist believing in separation, for example, of different ethnic groups

skinheads racists who hate nonwhite people and usually shave their heads and wear lace-up boots, jeans, and racist tattoos. There are also antiracist skinheads.

stereotypes negative ideas about a whole group of people, not based on fact, for example, that "all Muslims are terrorists"

suicide bombers people who wear explosives and go to a public place, where they blow themselves up along with others around them. They consider it to be a political action against an enemy government.

transnational corporation a company that operates in many countries

verbal abuse calling someone insulting names or shouting at him or her

welfare system the government system in many countries under which people who do not have enough money to live on are helped with money, housing, and services

FURTHER READING

Andryszewski, Tricia. *Immigration: Newcomers and Their Impact on the United States.* Brooklyn, N.Y.: Millbrook, 1995.

Cooper, Adrian. *Face the Facts: Racism.* Chicago: Raintree, 2003.

Grant, R.G. *20th Century Issues: Racism.* Chicago: Raintree, 2000.

Roleff, Tamara L. *Extremist Groups.* Farmington Hills, Mich.: Gale Group, 2001.

USEFUL ADDRESSES

American Civil Liberties Union (ACLU)
125 Broad Street, 18th Floor
New York, NY 10004

Anti-Racist Action Network (ARA)
P.O. Box 5688
Richmond, VA 23220

NAACP
4805 Mt. Hope Drive
Baltimore, Maryland 21215

Project Equality
7132 Main Street
Kansas City, MO 64114-1406

INDEX

INDEX